COLOR YOUR FEELINGS & EMOTIONS

RELAXATION & STRESS RELIEF COLORING BOOK

READ IT BEFORE YOU START COLORING
HERE ARE SOME TIPS THAT WILL HELP YOU

FIRST AND FOREMOST, AT THE END OF THIS BOOK YOU CAN FIND COLOR TEST PAGE. PLEASE, USE IT TO CHECK YOUR PENCILS AND MARKERS. TO AVOID SPOILAGE OF COLORING PAGES IN CASE OF USE OF MARKERS, THERE ARE SOME PAGES AT THE END OF THIS BOOK THAT YOU CAN PUT UNDER THE PAGE THAT YOU ARE PLANING TO COLOR.

AND FINALLY - ENJOY COLORING THESE PAGES!!! GOOD LUCK AND THANK YOU FOR CHOOSING THIS COLORING BOOK!!!

RELAXATION & STRESS RELIEF COLORING BOOK
30+ HIGH QUALITY ILLUSTRATIONS

I
WISH
YOU

LOVE

FREEDOM

SMILE

TRUST

WISDOM

SILENCE

RISK

FUN

HAPPINESS

CARE

INSPIRATION

DIGNITY

RELATIONSHIP

FAMILY

FRIENDSHIP

JOY

HOME

LAUGHTER

CONFIDIENCE

CREATIVITY

LUCK

HUMILITY

GENEROSITY

VIRTUE

ROMANCE

KINDNESS

TENDERNESS

HONOR

MODESTY

CALMNESS

▲ CUT THIS PAGE OUT OF THE BOOK AND USE IT UNDER THE PAGE YOU ARE COLORING TO PREVENT SPOILAGE OF THE NEXT PAGE

COLOR CHECK PAGE

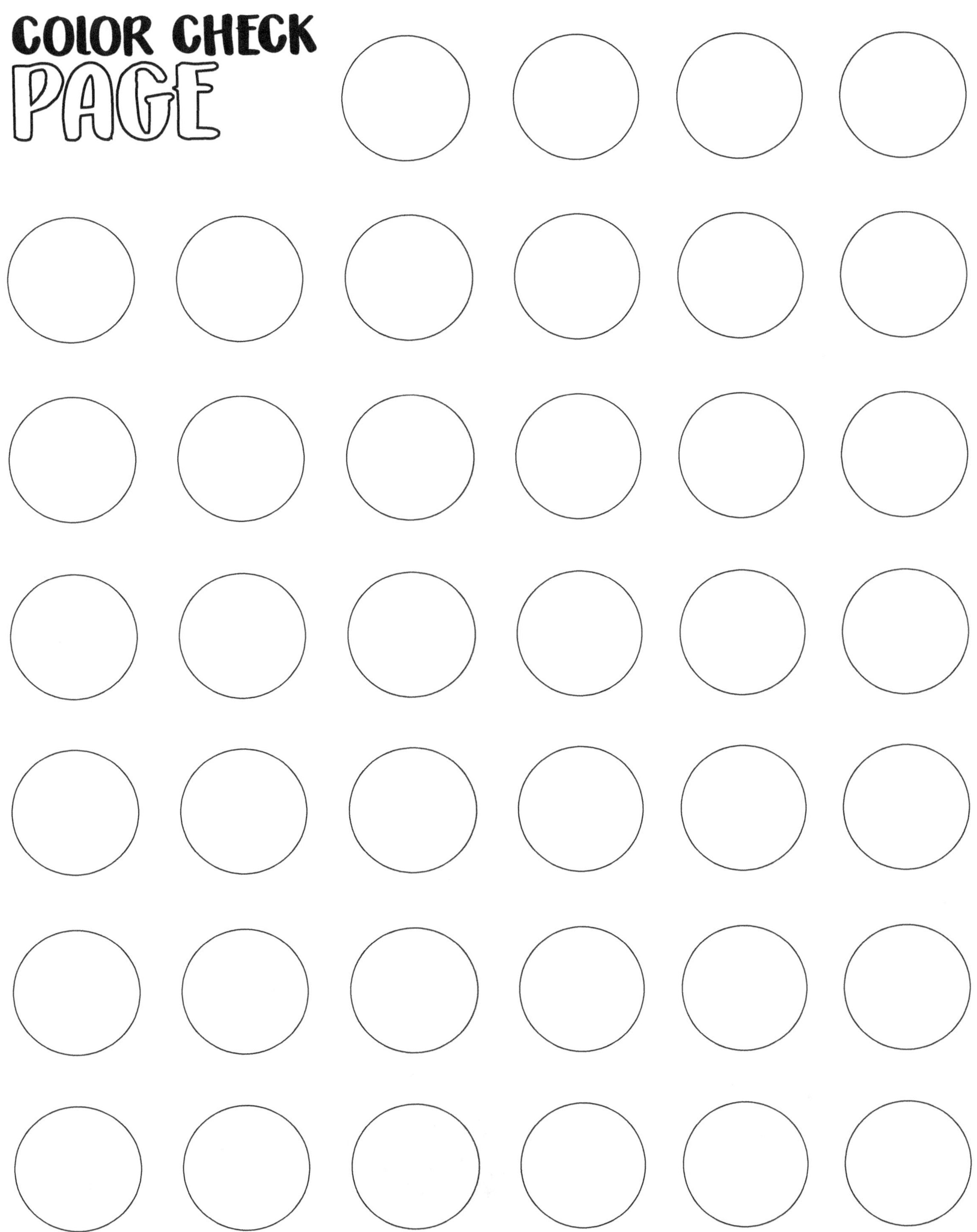